This book belongs to

_____

This Is Me
And My
Single Parent

*A Discovery Workbook for
Children and Single Parents*

by
Marla D. Evans

Magination Press
New York

DEDICATION
To my dear family,
John Steadman Rice,
Jesse Simone Rice-Evans,
Debbie Galusha and Kathleen Hall

THANKS TO
The Child Saving Institute Single Parent Support Group

ABOUT THE AUTHOR
Marla D. Evans has a graduate teaching certificate in education from
the University of California at Berkeley. Ms. Evans is author of
This Is Me and My Two Families.

ISBN 0-945354-17-7

Copyright © 1989 by Marla D. Evans

Published by Magination Press, an Imprint of Brunner/Mazel, Inc., 19 Union Square West, 8th Floor,
New York, NY 10003. *Distributed in the US by* Publishers Group West, 4065 Hollis, Emeryville, CA 94608.
Telephone 800-365-3453. In California call collect (414) 658-3453. *Distributed in Canada by* Book Center,
1140 Beaulac Street, Montreal, Quebec H4R 1R8.

MANUFACTURED IN THE UNITED STATES OF AMERICA

10 9 8 7 6 5 4 3 2 1

Table of Contents

A Note to the Parent

This discovery workbook focuses primarily on the interaction between a parent and a child of a single parent family. The goal of this workbook is to foster a new level of understanding between single parents and their children.

Participating together in this workbook will increase awareness and intimacy with one another and will increase the potential for long-term positive and effective communication. When working on this workbook together, it is important for the parent to encourage the child to express feelings openly, to engage in non-threatening dialogue and to listen attentively.

Although this workbook focuses primarily on one parent and child, other members of the family are referred to in various sections. The parent who is not living in the home with the single parent is referred to in a section entitled *My Other Parent*. The child may wish to own a copy of this workbook for each parent.

Placing primary focus on the single parent and child is not intended to diminish the importance of other family members in the child's life, but to help build a stronger foundation of understanding for one of the most important relationships of our lives—between parent and child.

If the child has two homes in which he or she lives, you may wish to purchase *This Is Me and My Two Families* (also published by Brunner/Mazel), which equally stresses family dynamics in the two households.

This workbook may be used in conjunction with a counselor or therapist.

A Few Helpful Words About This Discovery Workbook

- The parent and child should designate specific time, preferably uninterrupted, to work together on this workbook.

- Work on each page at the pace that is comfortable for both of you. This workbook is a process experience that requires time for both individuals to talk and listen to each other.

- This workbook is divided into categories which represent some of the main areas of focus in a child's life.

- Blank spaces are provided for the child's facts, feelings and opinions.

- There are sections that may be emotionally difficult for either the child or the parent. In some cases the participants may want to skip over some sections and return to work on them at a later point.

- Sentences and sections in the workbook that do not apply to the participants may be skipped.

- There are no right or wrong answers.

- Where necessary, instructions in parentheses are added beneath the blanks to more specifically guide the child.

- Where "My Parent" is noted, the child is encouraged to write the special name he/she uses for the single parent.

- The "Other Parent" section refers to the parent who is not the single parent focus of this book. The child may use the special name he/she uses for this parent.

- "Grandparents/Other Grandparents" allows for children to include their biological grandparents as well as adults they refer to as grandparents which can include grandparents of a half or step-sibling, or friends of the family.

- If the child is unable to write, the parent may do the writing for the child.

- Some categories in this book provide areas for drawings or photographs which reflect the child's perspective.

- This discovery workbook can be a highly rewarding experience for those involved in its process.

Descriptive Words Guide

You may use these words or find new descriptive words to use in your workbook.

alone	inadequate
angry	incapable
anxious	jealous
awful	joyful
bad	kind
beautiful	lazy
bored	loving
busy	marvelous
capable	mean
cheerful	miserable
comfortable	nice
confused	perfect
content	pleasant
curious	pleased
defeated	polite
depressed	protective
difficult	put down
disappointed	puzzled
discouraged	rejected
disrespect	respected
disruptive	sad
doubt	satisfied
drowsy	selfish
embarrassed	shame
excited	sick
fair	silly
fantastic	smart
friendly	special
frightened	strange
funny	strong
fussy	stupid
furious	surprised
good	terrible
great	threatening
grateful	tired
guilty	unfair
happy	unhappy
hate	unloved
helpful	useful
hopeful	weird
horrible	wild
hurt	wonderful
important	worried
	worthless

This Is Me

My History

My name is _____.

I was born on _____.
(what date)

I was born _____.
(in what hospital, in what town / city)

I weighed _____.
(how much)

My Mother's name is _____.

She was born _____.
(on what date, and in what town / city)

My Father's name is _____.

He was born _____.
(on what date, and in what town / city)

My parents stopped living together when I was _____
(how old)

because _____.

The way I feel about this is _____

because _____.

The person I talk to the most about this is _____.

I talk to this person because _____.

One of my best memories is _____

_____.

It is such a wonderful memory because _____

_____.

If I could change anything about my life, I would _____

_____

because _____.

This workbook is for _____ and I to work on together.
(which parent)

11

Life With Both My Parents In The Same Home

The way I felt about living in the same home with both my parents was _____

_____ .

I felt this way because _____ .

Some things I remember about us living together are _____

_____ .

I remember these things so well because _____

_____ .

Something I remember doing together with both my parents was _____

_____ .

I remember this so well because _____ .

When I think of my parents together, I think of _____

_____ .

When I think of this, I feel _____ .

The way I remember my parents treating each other was _____

_____ .

An example of them treating each other that way was when _____

_____ .

The way I felt about that was _____ .

The place I remember living most of the time with both my parents is _____ .

(describe what kind of home it was)

Some things I remember having in that home are _____

_____ .

The way I felt about that home is _____

because _____ .

The best thing about living with both my parents was _____

_____ .

It was so good because _____ .

The most difficult thing about living with my parents was _____

_____ .

It was so difficult because _____ .

If I could change something about my parents and I living together, I would _____
(change what)

_____ .

I would change this because _____

_____ .

My Parents Are Not Living Together Anymore

My parents have not been together _____ .
(for how long)

The way I feel about my parents not living together anymore is _____

_____ .

I feel this way because _____ .

The reason I think they decided not to live together anymore is _____

_____ .

The reason I think this is because _____ .

The way I feel about this is _____

_____ .

When I first found out that my parents were not going to live together anymore, I _____

_____ .
(what did you do, how did you act)

I acted this way, because I felt _____ .

I felt this way _____ .
(for how long)

I began to stop feeling this way when _____

_____ .

Since then, I have mostly felt _____
(how)

about my parents' divorce.

I have felt this way because _____ .

The person I have talked to the most about my parents is _____

_____ because _____ .

The way I have changed the most since my parents' divorce is _____

_____ .

The way _____ has changed the most since the divorce
(my parent with whom I'm doing this workbook)

is _____ .

The way I feel about that change is _____

because _____.

The way _____ has changed the most since the divorce
(my other parent)

is _____.

The way I feel about that change is _____

because _____.

The thing that has changed the most with the way we live is _____

_____.

I think this has happened because _____

_____.

The way I feel about this is _____

because _____.

The worst part about my parents not living together anymore is _____

_____.

I believe that my parents _____ get back together
(will, will not)

again because _____

_____.

_____ believes that _____ _____ get back
(My parent)   (he/she)   (will/will not)

together with _____ because _____
(my other parent)

_____.

_____ believes that _____ _____ get back
(My other parent)   (he/she)   (will/will not)

together with _____ because _____
(my parent)

_____.

Something I have learned from this experience is _____

_____.

Something I have learned about my parents is _____.

My Family

The names of the people in my family are _____

_____

_____

_____ .

I think my family is special because _____

_____ .

One person I do many things with in my family is _____ .

One thing we really love to do is _____ .

One thing I would like to change about my family is _____

_____ because _____ .

One thing I don't like about my family is _____

_____ .

I don't like this because _____ .

One thing I do like about my family is _____

_____ .

The people in my family usually treat each other _____

_____ .

I think they treat each other that way because _____

_____ .

There is _____ fighting in my family.

(how much)

Fights often happen because _____

_____ .

Fights usually end when _____

_____ .

The way I feel when I'm watching a fight is _____

_____.

The way I feel when I'm in a fight is _____

_____.

One of the best things my family did together was _____

_____.

It was so great because _____.

I know _____ other single parent families like my own.
(some, many, no)

I see my family as _____
(the same, somewhat different, very different)

compared to other families I know because _____

_____.

The way I feel about this is _____

_____.

I think being in a single parent family is _____
(better or worse than, the same as)

being in a two parent family because _____

_____.

Someday, when I have my own family, some things I will do differently from the one

I live in are _____

_____ because _____

Some things I would do the same are _____

_____.

This is my family. . .

My Brothers and Sisters / Half and Step Siblings

I have _____ _____ .
　　　　　　(how many)　　　　　　　　　　　　(brothers and sisters – half / step siblings)

The _____ I spend the most time with is _____ .
　　　　　(which siblings)

The way we spend much of our time together is _____ .

One of the best things I ever did with _____ was
　　　　　　　　　　　　　　　　　　　　　(which siblings)

_____ .

One of the worst things I ever did with _____ was
　　　　　　　　　　　　　　　　　　　　　(which sibling)

_____ .

The way _____ felt about my parents getting a divorce was
　　　　　　　　　　(which sibling)

The way that _____ feel/s now about the divorce
　　　　　　　　　　　　(which sibling/s)

is/are _____

because _____ .

_____ talk about my parents getting a divorce _____ .
　　　(Which sibling/s)　　　　　　　　　　　　　　　　　　　　　　　(how often)

The way that life for my _____ has changed since my parents' divorce is _____
　　　　　　　　　　　　(which sibling/s)

_____ .

The way they feel about that is _____ .

They believe that the reason this change happened is because _____

_____ .

Something that _____ _____ learned since my parents' divorce
　　　　　　　　　(which sibling/s)　　　　　(has / have)

is _____ .

_____ and I talk about the way we feel with
　　　　　　　　(Which sibling/s)

each other _____ because _____
　　　　　　　　　　(how often)

_____ .

19

What I Think of Myself

I think I am a _____ person.

I think I am this kind of person because _____

_____.

I show others I am this kind of person by _____
(what do you do)

_____.

One thing I like about myself is _____

because _____.

One thing I do not like about myself is _____

because _____.

I could make this better by _____.

If I could change one thing about the way I think and feel, I would change _____

_____ because _____.

One way I could change this thing is by _____

_____.

When I look in the mirror, I see a person who is _____

_____.

I feel _____ about the way I look because _____

_____.

If I could change one thing about the way I look, I would change _____

_____ because _____.

One way I could change this thing is by _____

_____.

What I Think of My Parent

I think _____ is _____.
        (my parent)

I think _____ is this because _____.
        (my parent)

_____ looks _____.
        (My parent)

One of the best things about _____ is _____

_____ because _____.

One thing I wish _____ would change is _____

_____ because _____.

I've wished this for _____
                                              (how long)

One thing _____ did to surprise me was _____

_____.

It surprised me because _____.

Something I think _____ would like to change about me is _____
                 (my parent)

_____ because

_____.

Something I think _____ would like to change about _____
                 (my parent)   (himself / herself)

is _____ because

_____.

I think one of _____ favorite things to do is _____
             (my parent's)

_____ because _____.

The way I feel about _____ favorite thing is _____
                    (his / her)

because _____.

I think one of _____ least favorite things to do is _____
(my parent's)

_____ because _____ .

The way _____ feels about being a single parent is _____
(my parent)

_____

_____ .

_____ has been a single parent for _____
(My parent)   (how long)

I think that life for _____ is _____
(my parent)   (how easy or difficult)

because _____ .

I help _____ by _____
(my parent)   (doing what)

because _____ .

I think _____ believes that life would be better if _____
(my parent)

_____ .

I think this is because _____

_____ .

My Other Parent

I understand my _____ _____.
(special name for this parent)   (very well, some, not at all)

I understand _____ _____ because _____
(him / her)   (very well, some, not at all)

_____.

I feel _____ about this because _____.

Some things I know about _____ are _____
(this parent)

_____

_____.

The way I found these things out was _____

_____.

Some things I wish I knew about _____ are _____
(this parent)

_____.

I wish to know these things because _____.

I feel _____ because I don't know these things.

I _____ _____ because _____
(how do you feel about)   (this parent)

_____.

I see _____ _____.
(this parent)   (how much of the time)

I feel _____ about how much I see _____ because
(him / her)

_____.

Some things we do together are _____

_____.

One thing I really like about _____ is _____
(this parent)

23

_____ because _____ .

One thing I do not like about _____ is _____
(this parent)

_____ because _____ .

_____   _____ me because _____
(This parent)   (how does he / she feel about you)

_____ .

Some things _____ thinks about me are _____
(this parent)

_____ .

_____ thinks these things because _____ .
(He / She)

I feel these things are _____ because
(true, partially true, false)

_____ .

If I could make a wish about my parents, I would wish _____

_____ .

If I could make a wish about _____ ,
(special name for this parent)

I would wish _____ .

If I could change anything about this parent, _____
(what would you change)

_____

because _____ .

If I could change anything about what this parent and I do together, _____
(what would you change)

_____ .

If I could say anything to _____ , I would say _____
(this parent)

_____ .

If I could make a wish about _____ and I, I would wish
(this parent)

_____ .

This is me and _____ . . .
(my other parent)

My Grandparents/Other Grandparents

My grandparents' names are _____

_____

_____

_____.

The parents of _____ live _____.
           (my parent)   (where)

I see them _____.
                  (how frequently)

The way I feel about seeing them is _____

because _____.

If I could make one wish about these grandparents, I would wish _____

_____

because _____.

The parents of _____ live _____.
           (my other parent)   (where)

I see them _____.
                  (how frequently)

The way I feel about seeing them is _____

because _____.

Of all my grandparents, I spend most of my time with _____
                                (which grandparent)

_____ because _____.

The way I feel about this is _____.

What we like to do together is _____.

One very important thing _____ taught me was _____
            (which grandparent)

_____.

This is so important because _____.

One thing I've taught _____ is _____.
           (which grandparent)

The way I feel about being old is _____.

My Friends

Friends are _____ .
(your definition)

The way I feel about having friends is _____

because _____ .

I spend _____ of my time with friends _____
(how much)   (what kinds of things do you and your friends do)

_____ .

_____ feels _____ about my friends because _____
(My parent)   (how)

_____ .

One thing _____ has said about my friends is _____
(my parent)

_____ .

_____ of my friends also live in single parent families.
(How many)

The way I feel about having friends from single parent families is _____

because _____ .

Being a friend means _____ .

It is _____ to be a friend.
(how easy or how hard)

I make friends _____ because _____ .
(how easily)

Things I can do to make new friends are _____ .

My best friend is _____ .

We have been friends for _____ .
(how long)

We are best friends because _____ .

I like _____ so much because _____ .
(him / her)

Sometimes we disagree about _____ .

We finish disagreeing when _____ .

Here I am with my best friend. . .

My Parent

My Parent's History

The names of _____ brothers and sisters are _____
                 (my parent's)   (my aunts and uncles)

_____

_____ .

The way _____ describes growing up is _____
        (my parent)

_____ .

The way _____ describes her mother is _____
        (my parent)

_____ .

The way _____ describes her father is _____
        (my parent)

_____ .

Other important adults _____ grew up spending time with
                     (my parent)

were _____ .

One of _____ best memories of growing up is _____
      (my parent's)

_____ .

One of the hardest parts about growing up to _____ was
                                   (my parent)

_____ .

One thing _____ wants to see happen differently in my life
           (my parent)

than in _____ own is _____
     (his/her)

because _____ .

Here is _____ family when
                    (my parent's)

_____ was growing up...
      (he / she)

What My Parent Thinks of Himself/Herself

_____ thinks _____ is _____ .
(My parent)   (he/she)   (what kind of person)

_____ thinks this because _____ .
(He/She)

_____ shows that _____ is this kind of person by _____
(He/She)   (he/she)

_____ .
(what does he/she do to show this)

_____ thinks _____ life is _____
(My parent)   (his/her)   (description)

because _____ .

_____ feels _____ about being a parent.
(My parent)

_____ feels _____ about being a single
(My parent)

parent because _____ .

If _____ could do anything in the world, _____ would
     (my parent)   (he/she)

_____ because _____ .

One thing _____ would like to change about the way _____
              (my parent)   (he/she)

thinks or feels is _____

because _____ .

_____ thinks _____ looks _____ .
(My parent)   (he/she)

One thing _____ would like to change about the way _____
              (my parent)   (he/she)

looks is _____ because _____ .

One thing _____ likes about _____ is_____
              (my parent)   (himself/herself)

_____ .

One thing _____ does not like about _____ is
              (my parent)   (himself/herself)

_____ because _____ .

_____ thinks other people _____
(My parent)   (how does your parent think others feel about him/her.)

_____ thinks this because _____ .
(He/She)

33

Something _____ wishes others understood about _____
(my parent)   (him / her)
is _____ .

_____ wishes this because _____ .
(He / She)

If I could change one thing about the way _____ feels about _____ ,
(my parent)   (himself / herself)
it would be _____

_____ .

I want to change this because _____

_____ .

If _____ could change one thing about _____ life, _____
(my parent)   (his / her)   (he/she)
would change _____ .

_____ would change this because _____
(He / She)

_____ .

One thing _____ would always keep the same is _____
(my parent)
_____ because _____

_____ .

What My Parent Thinks of Me

_____ thinks I am _____.
(My parent)

_____ thinks this because _____.
(He / She)

I believe that _____ is _____ about
(my parent)   (right, somewhat right, wrong)

this because _____.

One positive thing _____ thinks about me is _____.
(my parent)

One thing _____ wishes I would change about myself is _____
(my parent)

_____ because _____.

What I feel about that wish is _____.

_____ approves of what I do _____.
(My parent)   (how much of the time)

_____ shows approval by _____.
(He / She)

When _____ shows approval, I feel _____.
(he / she)

When my parent disapproves of me, I feel _____.

_____ shows disapproval by _____.
(He / She)

The kinds of things _____ mostly disapproves of are _____.
(he / she)

_____ because _____.

If _____ could change anything about the way I think and feel, _____
(my parent)   (he / she)

would change _____ because _____.

The way I feel about this is _____.

_____ feels _____ about the way I look because _____
(My parent)

_____.

If my parent could change anything about the way I look, _____ would change
(he / she)

_____ because _____.

The way I feel about this is _____.

35

Working For a Living

_____ works because _____ .
(My parent)

_____ works _____ and has worked there _____ .
(He / She)　　　　　　(where)　　　　　　　　　　　　　　　　　　(how long)

_____ _____ to work there because _____ .
(He / She)　(likes, doesn't like)

_____ .

I know this because _____ .

One thing I know about what _____ does at work is _____ .
(my parent)

_____ .

One thing _____ likes about _____ job is _____ .
(my parent)　　　　　　(his / her)

because _____ .

One thing _____ doesn't like about _____ job is_____ .
(my parent)　　　　　　　　　(his / her)

_____ .

My opinion of _____ job is _____ .
(my parent's)

because _____ .

Most of the time when _____ comes home from work _____ .
(my parent)　　　　　　　　　　　　　　　　　　(he / she)

seems to feel _____ .

If _____ could do any job in the world, _____ would_____ .
(my parent)　　　　　　　　　　　　　　　(he / she)

_____ because _____ .

I know this because _____ .

The work I would like to do when I grow up is _____ .

_____ because _____ .

To prepare myself to do that work, I must _____ .

_____ .

36

Here is _____ at work. . .
(my parent)

37

My Parent's Friends

_____ thinks having friends is _____ because
     (My parent)   (how important)

_____ .

Some things _____ does with _____ friends are _____
          (my parent)   (his / her)

_____ .

One thing _____ likes about _____ best friend is _____
        (my parent)   (his / her)

_____

I feel _____ about _____ best friend
                                        (my parent's)

because _____ .

Friends of _____ who help take care of me are _____
          (my parent's)

_____ .

_____ friends help take care of me _____ .
     (His / her)   (how often)

The way I feel about _____ friends helping to take care of me is _____
                    (my parent's)

_____ .

_____ asks _____ friends to help take care of me when _____
  (My parent)   (his / her)   (the parent)

_____ .
                                  (is doing what)

The way _____ feels about _____ and I being friends is _____
        (my parent)   (he / she — the parent)

_____ .

The way _____ divorce changed our own relationship is _____
        (my parents')   (how)

_____ .

The way we both feel about that change is _____

_____ .

Dating

A date is _____ .

_____ goes on dates _____ .
           (My parent)   (how often)

_____ feels _____ about dating because _____
(My parent)   (how)

_____ .

The way I feel about _____ dating is _____
                          (my parent)

_____ because _____ .

When _____ tells me _____ is going out, I _____
         (my parent)   (he / she)

_____ because _____ .

I feel _____ about the _____ _____
                                     (people / person)   (my parent)

dates because _____ .

When _____ is on a date, I _____ .
         (my parent)   (what do you do)

When _____ is on a date, I feel _____
         (my parent)

because _____ .

I think _____ wants to go out because _____
         (my parent)

_____ .

It is important for _____ to go out sometimes because _____
           (my parent)

_____ .

If I could change one thing about _____ dating, I would change _____
                                        (my parent)

_____ .

I talk to _____ _____ about _____ dating.
         (my parent)   (how often)   (his / her)

I feel _____ about talking about it because _____

_____ .

Us

My Single Parent and I

Some ways _____ and I are the most alike are _____
(my parent)

_____ .

The way I feel about these things is _____

_____ .

The reason I think we are so much alike in these areas is _____

_____ .

Some ways that _____ and I are different are _____
(my parent)

_____ .

The way I feel about these differences is _____

_____ .

The reason I think we are so different in these ways is because _____

_____ .

The way I feel about living in a single parent family is _____

_____ because _____ .

The way _____ feels about our single parent family is _____
(he / she)

_____ because _____ .

Something we love to do together is _____ .

We love to do this because _____ .

One area of difficulty for us is _____ .

It is difficult because _____ .

We usually handle difficulties between us by _____
(what do you do)

_____ .

If I could change one thing about the relationship between _____ and I, I would
(my parent)

change _____ .

This is _____ and I . . .
(my parent)

Talking

I feel _____ about talking because _____.

Some things I like to talk about are _____
_____.

I like to talk about these things because _____
_____.

Some things I don't like to talk about are _____
_____.

I don't like to talk about them because _____
_____.

_____ feels _____ about talking because _____
(My parent)
_____.

Some things _____ loves to talk about are _____
(he / she)
_____ because _____.

Some things _____ doesn't like to talk about are _____
(he / she)
_____ because _____.

_____ and I talk together _____. I feel _____
(My parent)   (how often)
about talking that much because _____.

One thing I would like to talk to _____ about is _____
(my parent)
_____ because _____.

Someone I talk to a lot is _____.

A person _____ talks to the most is _____.
(my parent)

I _____ like to talk about the way I feel because _____
(do, don't, sometimes)
_____.

_____ _____ to talk about the way that _____ feels
(My parent)   (likes, dislikes)   (he / she)
because _____.

45

Here, _____ and I are talking...
(my parent)

Listening

I am _____ interested in listening to others
(always, sometimes, not)

because _____ .

I _____ like it when people listen to me
(always, sometimes, never)

because _____ .

When I listen to people, I feel _____ .

When people listen to me, I feel _____ .

My parent listens to me _____ .
(sometimes, all the time)

When _____ listens to me, I feel _____ .
(he / she)

I listen to my parent _____ .
(sometimes, all the time)

When I don't listen to my parent, _____ _____ .
(he / she)   (feels how)

When _____ doesn't listen to me, I feel _____
(my parent)

because _____ .

The way I try to get _____ to listen to me is _____
(him / her)

_____ .

It _____ works because _____ .
(never, sometimes, always)

Something I could tell _____ to let _____ know I'd like
(my parent)   (him / her)

to be listened to is _____

_____ .

Something _____ could tell me to let me know _____ would
(my parent)   (he / she)

like to be listened to is _____

_____ .

Sharing

I feel that sharing is _____ because _____
                          (how important)

_____ .

It is _____ for me to share with others because
      (how easy or hard)

_____ .

I share _____ .
        (how often)

One thing I like to share with _____ is _____
                               (my parent)

_____ because _____ .

One thing _____ likes to share with me is _____
          (my parent)

_____ because _____ .

One thing I don't like to share with anyone is _____

_____ because _____ .

The one thing I need to share more of is _____

because _____ .

Knowing when to share and when not to share is important because _____

_____ .

One thing I wish _____ would share with me is _____
                 (my parent)

_____ because _____ .

I feel _____ when people share things with me because

_____ .

_____ feels that sharing is _____
(My parent)

because _____ .

48

Time

I _____ enough time to do what I want to do because _____
      (have / don't have)

_____ .

_____ _____ a lot of time to do what _____
     (My parent)   (has / doesn't have)   (he / she)

wants to do because _____ .

When I have free time, I usually spend it _____ .
                                                    (doing what)

When _____ has free time, _____ usually spends it _____
     (my parent)   (he / she)   (doing what)

_____ .

I like to make time _____
                                         (to do what)

because _____ .

I don't like to make time to _____

because _____ .

I organize my time _____ .
                            (how well)

I _____ having free time because _____
   (how do you feel)

_____ .

What _____ and I usually do when we spend time together is _____
    (my parent)

_____ .

The way I feel about this is _____ .

When I want to spend more time with _____ , and there is not
                                           (my parent)

enough time, _____ .
                                     (what happens)

When _____ wants to spend more time with me, and there is not
                   (my parent)

enough time, _____ .

If I could change anything about time, I'd change _____ .

Thinking

The thing I think about the most is _____

because _____.

The thing I like to think about the most is _____

_____ because _____.

One thing I don't like to think about is _____

_____ because _____.

When I think about this thing, I _____.

(how do you behave)

To stop thinking this thought, I _____

_____.

Some thoughts I tell _____ about are _____

(my parent)

_____.

I tell _____ these things because _____

(him / her)

_____.

When I tell _____ these thoughts, _____ _____

(him / her)   (he / she)   (does what)

_____.

Some thoughts _____ tells me are _____

(my parent)

_____.

The way I feel when _____ tells me these things is _____

(he / she)

_____.

Dreams

Dreams are _____.

I remember my dreams _____.

(how often)

One of my favorite dreams was _____

_____.

I liked it so much because _____

_____.

A dream I didn't like was _____.

It bothered me because _____.

I talk to _____ about my dreams.

_____ remembers _____ dreams _____.

(My parent)   (his / her)   (how much of the time)

One of _____ favorite dreams was _____

(his / her)

_____.

_____ liked it so much because _____

(He / She)

_____.

A dream _____ didn't like at all was _____.

(he / she)

It was a bad dream because _____.

If I could pick a dream to live in for a while, I would pick _____

_____ because _____

_____.

If _____ could pick a dream to live in for a while, _____ would pick _____

(my parent)   (he / she)

_____

because _____.

This is a picture of one of my dreams...

Wishes

It is _____ for people to have wishes because _____
            (how important)
_____ .

One wish I want to come true is _____
_____ .

I want this wish to come true because _____
_____ .

One thing I can do to help my wish come true is _____
_____ .

_____ wishes that someday _____
     (My parent)
_____ .

_____ has been wishing this ever since _____
     (He / She)
_____ .

One wish I have told _____ about is _____
                        (my parent)
_____ .

One reason I think some peoples' wishes don't come true is because _____
_____ .

One reason why _____ thinks some peoples' wishes don't come true is because _____
                (my parent)
_____ .

53

Discipline

Discipline means _____ .

The way I feel about discipline is _____

because _____ .

I usually get disciplined when _____ .

The kind of discipline I usually get is _____

_____ .

The person who usually disciplines me the most is _____ .

The way I feel when I get disciplined is _____ .

I get disciplined _____ .
                          (how often)

Most of the time, I think the discipline I receive is _____
                                                          (how fair)

because _____ .

The way _____ acts before _____ disciplines me is _____
           (my parent)   (he/she)

_____ .

The way _____ acts after _____ disciplines me is _____
           (my parent)   (he/she)

_____ .

The way I usually act after I get disciplined is _____ .

The way I feel after I get disciplined is _____ .

After I get disciplined, it takes me about _____ to feel OK.
                                                  (how long)

After being disciplined, _____ and I talk about what happened _____
                            (my parent)   (how often)

_____ .

After we talk, we both feel _____ .

If I could discipline one person, I would discipline _____
                                                         (whom)

because _____ .

Money

To me, money is _____ .
                          (how important)

I feel this way because _____ .

_____ feels money is _____ .
   (My parent)   (how important)

_____ thinks this because _____ .
   (He / She)

I think my family _____ .
                          (is wealthy, has a medium amount of $, is poor)

The way I feel about that is _____

because _____ .

_____ feels that we are _____ .
   (My parent)   (wealthy, have a medium amount of $, is poor)

The way _____ feels about that is _____
           (he / she)

because _____ .

The way our family gets money is _____ .

Some things money can buy are _____

_____ .

Some things money can't buy are _____

_____ .

To get money, I have to _____ .

For _____ to get money, _____ has to _____ .
    (my parent)   (he / she)

The way _____ feels about this is _____ .
           (he / she)

When I am older, the way I would like to make my living is _____

_____ .

If _____ could make a living in the way that _____ would most like,
      (my parent)   (he / she)

_____ would _____ .
   (he / she)

Responsibility

I _____ to have responsibilities because _____
  (like, don't like)

_____.

One of my biggest responsibilities is _____.

It seems so big because _____.

I feel I have _____ responsibilities because
  (too few, just enough, too many)

_____.

Before my parents' divorce, I had _____ responsibilities
  (fewer, the same amount of, more)

than I do now because _____

_____.

The way I feel about this is _____.

Compared to my friends, I have _____ responsibilities
  (fewer, the same amount of, more)

than they because _____.

I think _____ has _____ responsibilities
  (my parent)   (few, just enough, too many)

because _____.

The way I feel about the amount of things _____ feels _____
  (he / she)   (he / she)

must do is _____.

The way _____ feels about _____ amount of responsibilities
  (he / she)   (his / her)

is _____.

The kid in the family who has the most responsibility for the other kids is _____.

The way _____ feels about that is _____.
  (he / she)

If I could change anything about my responsibilities, I'd _____

_____.

Emotions

Happiness

Being happy means _____.

I feel _____ happy most of the time because _____
      (how)

_____.

When I am happy, I feel _____ because _____

_____.

When I am happy, the world seems _____.

I feel _____ when _____ is happy.
     (how)   (my parent)

_____ is very happy when _____
  (My parent)

because _____.

I can see that _____ is happy because _____.
        (he / she)

I am very happy when _____ because

_____.

I show that I am happy by _____.

_____ is happy when I _____
  (My parent)   (do what)

because _____.

I am happy when _____ _____
      (my parent)   (does what)

because _____.

When I want _____ to be happy, I_____
      (my parent)

When _____ wants me to be happy, _____ _____.
    (my parent)   (he / she)

I would be the happiest person in the world if _____

_____.

_____ would be the happiest person in the world if _____
  (My parent)

_____.

I am very happy here. . .

Fear

I am _____ afraid.
        (never, sometimes, often)

When I am afraid, I feel _____ because _____.

I stop being afraid when _____.

One thing that I felt very afraid about was _____

_____ because _____.

One thing that I am afraid to think about is _____

because _____.

_____ is _____ afraid.
    (My parent)   (never, sometimes, often)

One thing I know _____ is afraid about is _____
        (my parent)

_____.

_____ is afraid of this because _____.
(He / She)

The way _____ stops being afraid is _____.
    (he / she)

_____ doesn't like to be afraid because _____.
(He / She)

One thing I learned about being afraid is _____

_____.

When someone I care about is afraid, I _____
        (what do you do for that person)

_____ because _____.

If I could make one wish for one fear to go away, I would wish _____

_____.

because _____.

Jealousy

Jealousy means _____ .

I feel jealous _____ .
                            (how often)

One thing that I most often feel jealous about is _____

_____ .

I think I feel jealous when that happens because _____

_____ .

The way I feel inside when I am jealous is _____ .

What I do when I feel jealous is _____ .

Something I think, do or say to feel less jealous about this is _____

_____ .

I talk to _____ about being jealous.
                            (whom)

I talk to this person because _____ .

I _____ tell _____ when I feel jealous.
        (how often)   (my parent)

When I talk to _____ about this, _____ _____
                 (my parent)   (he / she)

_____ .

I feel _____ after I talk to _____ about this because
                 (how)   (my parent)

_____ .

A positive thing that has come out of my feeling jealous is _____

_____ .

The one thing I'd like to never feel jealous about again is _____

_____ .

Love

I show love to _____ by _____ .
(my parent)   (what do you do?)

_____ shows love to me by _____ .
(My parent)

When I show love to _____ , I feel _____
(my parent)

because _____ .

When I receive love from _____ , I feel _____
(my parent)

because _____ .

I feel I am loved _____ because _____ .
(a little, some, a lot)

Sometimes I feel unloved when _____ .
(what happens for you to feel unloved)

I start feeling loved again when _____ .

My parents feel loved _____ .
(a little, some, a lot)

I know this because _____ .

One thing _____ told me about love is _____ .
(my parent)

Feeling love towards myself means _____ .

I _____ love myself because _____
(do, sometimes, do not)

_____ .

_____ _____ loves _____ .
(My parent)   (always, sometimes, never)   (himself / herself)

I know this because _____ .

The way I feel about this is _____ .

Loving yourself is _____ important because
(a little, somewhat, very)

_____ .

Anger

Anger is _____.

I get angriest when _____.

I show I'm angry by _____.

I stop being angry when _____.

_____ gets angriest when _____
(My parent)

_____.

_____ shows _____ angry by _____
(My parent)   (he's / she's)

_____ stops being angry when _____
(My parent)

When others see me angry, they _____.

When _____ is angry, I _____.
(my parent)

I feel _____ when _____ is angry because _____
(my parent)

_____.

When I get angry, _____ feels _____ because
(my parent)

_____.

Sometimes when I am angry inside, I don't show it because _____

_____.

I feel _____ after I am finished being angry because _____

_____.

When _____ and I are finished being angry at each other, we _____
(my parent)

_____.

_____ and I _____ discuss our fights. We do this because
(My parent)   (how often)

_____.

After discussing our fights, we both feel _____

because _____.

_____ and I are angry here. . .
(My parent)

Sadness

I get sad _____ .
(how often)

I mostly get sad about _____ .

I think I get sad about this because _____

_____ .

The way I act when I get sad is _____ .

I know why I'm sad _____ .
(how much of the time)

I mostly talk to _____ about why I'm sad.
(whom)

What I do, think or say to be less sad is _____ .

_____ gets sad _____ .
(My parent)   (how often)

_____ mostly gets sad about _____ .
(He / She)

_____ shows _____ sad by _____ .
(He / She)   (he's / she's)   (how does he / she act)

When I'm sad, _____ _____ .
(my parent)   (what does he / she do)

When that happens, I feel _____ because

_____ .

When _____ gets sad, I _____ .
(my parent)   (how do you act or feel)

_____ usually seems to stop being sad when _____
(My parent)

_____ .

I _____ being sad because _____ .
(how do you feel)

One positive thing that came out of being sad once is _____

_____ .

Everybody gets sad _____ .
(about how often in your opinion)

66

Trust

Trusting someone means _____ .

It is _____ for me to trust people.
     (how easy or hard)

I trust _____ people.
     (about how many)

Trusting some people is _____ because _____
     (how important)

_____ .

The people I trust most are _____ .
     (whom)

The reasons I trust them are _____ .

Some people who trust me are _____ .
     (whom)

They trust me because _____ .

The way I feel knowing some people trust me is _____

_____ .

The person I trust most in the world is _____

because _____ .

_____ trusts that I will _____ .
     (My parent)   (do what)

If I don't do what _____ trusts me to do, _____
     (my parent)   (what happens)

_____ .

I trust _____ to _____ .
     (my parent)   (do what)

If _____ doesn't do what I trust _____ will do, _____
     (he / she)   (he / she)

_____   _____ .
     (what happens)   (and how do you feel)

The person I do not trust is _____ .

because _____ .

Hurting

Being hurt means _____.

When people are hurt, they feel _____.

When I see a person who is hurt, I feel _____.

When I am hurt, I feel _____.

When I am hurt, I want _____ to _____.
                               (my parent)

I want this because _____.

When my parent is hurt, I _____.
                                                 (what do you do)

When I do this, _____ feels _____.
                (he/she)

Once I felt very hurt when _____

_____.

The way I stopped feeling hurt was _____

_____.

What I learned from that experience was _____

_____.

The way _____ usually stops feeling hurt is _____
           (my parent)

_____.

The person I talk to about feeling hurt is _____.

I talk to this person because _____.

When I hurt someone else's feelings, I _____
                                          (what do you do; do you walk away, talk to them, etc.)

_____.

When I hurt someone else's feelings, I feel _____

because _____.

I can usually tell that I have hurt someone's feelings by _____

_____.

Guilt

I feel guilty _____ .
(how often)

The thing I feel guiltiest about is _____ .

I feel so guilty about this because _____

_____ .

The way _____ feels about feeling guilty is _____
(my parent)

_____ .

When I feel guilty, I feel _____ inside.
(how)

To stop feeling this way, I _____ .

For _____ to stop feeling guilty, _____ _____
(my parent)   (he/she)   (does what)

_____ .

When I feel guilty, I act _____
(how do you spend your time when you are feeling guilty)

_____ .

The way I feel about spending my time that way is _____

_____ .

I know the things that I will feel guilty about _____ .
(how much of the time)

The way I feel about blaming others for the things I have or have not done is _____

_____ .

I usually blame _____ when I feel guilty because _____
(whom)

_____ .

Taking responsibility for my actions is _____
(how important)

because _____ .

The next time I do or don't do something I know I will feel guilty about, I _____

_____ .

Our Home

Our Home

The way I describe our home is _____

_____ .

I feel _____ about our home because _____
          (how)

_____ .

What I like most about my home is _____

_____ .

What I like least about my home is _____

_____ .

We have been living here _____ .
          (how long)

What _____ likes most about our home is _____
    (my parent)

_____ .

What _____ likes least about our home is _____
    (my parent)

_____ .

The way I describe my own room is _____

_____ .

The way I feel about my room is _____

When I'm alone in my room, I usually _____
          (do what)

_____ .

When I'm alone in the house, I usually _____
          (do what)

_____ .

When I'm alone in the house, I feel _____

because _____ .

I'm usually alone somewhere in the house _____ .
          (how much of the time)

If I could change anything about my room, I would change _____

_____

because _____ .

If _____ could change anything about our home, _____ would change
     (my parent)   (he / she)

_____

because _____ .

I feel like our home is special because _____

_____ .

I feel _____ bringing others to my home because _____

_____ .

If I could live anywhere in the world, I'd live _____
                                                       (where)

_____ .

I would like to live there because _____

_____ .

I would like to live there with _____ because
                                               (whom)

_____ .

This is my home. . .

Chores

I _____ doing chores because _____.
(like, sometimes like, hate)

I think I am expected to do _____ chores
(too few, just enough, too many)

because _____.

_____ does _____ of chores because _____
(My parent)   (a few, some, a lot)

_____.

_____ feels _____ about doing chores because _____
(He / She)

_____.

I feel the amount of chores _____ does is _____ because
(he / she)   (fair, unfair)

_____.

I feel the amount of chores I do is _____ because _____
(fair, unfair)

_____.

The way I know the chores I am supposed to do and when I am supposed to do them is _____

_____.

When I don't do the chores I am expected to do, _____
(what happens)

_____.

When _____ doesn't do the chores _____ is expected to do,
(my parent)   (he / she)

_____.
(what happens)

Doing chores is _____ important because _____
(very, sometimes, not)

_____.

If I could do the chores I want to do when I want to do them, I would _____
(what would you do, when)

_____.

If my parent could do the chores _____ wants to do when _____
(he / she)   (he / she)

wants to do them, _____ would _____.
(he / she)   (what chores would be done when)

76

Eating

I _____ to eat because _____.
(how do you feel)

The foods I eat the most are _____

_____.

The way _____ feels about food is _____.
(my parent)

_____ feels this way because _____.
(He/She)

My favorite meal is _____ because _____

_____.

My least favorite meal is _____ because _____.

_____ favorite meal is _____
(My parent's)

because _____.

_____ least favorite meal is _____
(My parent's)

because _____.

The person who prepares most of the food in our family is _____

because _____.

The person who sets the table the most is _____

because _____.

The person who does the dishes the most is _____

because _____.

My family sits down together for meals _____.
(how often)

When I eat meals with my family, we _____.
(what do you do during)

One of the most unhealthy foods for me to eat is _____.

Holidays

The way I feel about holidays is _____ .

I usually spend holidays _____ .
(where)

My favorite holiday is _____

because _____ .

I like it so much because _____ .

_____ favorite holiday is _____
(My parent's)

because _____ .

My least favorite holiday is _____

because _____ .

_____ least favorite holiday is _____
(My parent's)

because _____ .

The way I feel after my favorite holiday is over is _____

_____ because _____ .

The way _____ feels after _____ favorite holiday is
(my parent)   (his/her)

over is _____ because _____ .

The best holiday I ever remember was _____ .

It was so wonderful because _____ .

The best holiday _____ remembers was _____ .
(my parent)

It was so wonderful because _____

_____ .

If I could invent a holiday, it would be _____ .

The people who would celebrate this holiday with me are _____

_____ . Some of the things we would do are

_____ .

Here is my family on my favorite holiday. . .

Visitors

Some people who come to see us are _____.

I feel _____ about people coming to visit my home.
       (how)

One thing I like about having people visit is _____

_____ because _____.

One thing I don't like about having people visit is _____

_____ because _____.

The way _____ feels about having visitors is _____
        (my parent)

_____ because _____.

Most of the people who visit our home come to see _____.
                                                    (whom)

When people come to visit _____, I _____.
                          (my parent)   (what do you do)

I feel _____ about doing that because _____.
       (how)

When people come to visit me, _____ _____.
                              (my parent)   (does what)

The way I feel about that is _____

because _____.

The person we visit the most is _____ because

_____.

_____ feels _____ about visiting that person
        (My parent)

because _____.

The person I visit the most is _____ because

_____.

The person I want to visit the most in the world is _____

_____ because _____.

Beyond Our Home

Relatives

Relatives are _____.

I see my relatives _____.
_____(how often)

I _____ seeing them because _____.
(like, dislike)

One relative I really like is _____ because

_____.

I see this person _____.
_____(how much of the time)

I feel _____ about seeing _____ that much because _____
(him/her)

_____.

Most of our relatives treat us _____
_____(how)

because _____.

We treat our relatives _____
_____(how)

because _____.

_____ feels _____ about relatives because _____
(My parent)

_____.

_____ talks to _____ the most because _____
(My parent)   (which relative)

_____.

_____ talks about _____ the most because _____.
(My parent)   (which relative)

One thing I love to do with _____ is _____.
(which relative)

The relative I feel closest to is _____ because _____

_____.

One relative I have trouble with is _____ because _____

_____.

If I could change anything about relatives, it would be _____

_____.

School

I feel that school is _____
                                    (how important)

because _____.

The way I feel about school is _____

because _____.

The way _____ feels about school is _____
                (my parent)

because _____.

The best thing about school is _____

because _____.

The worst thing about school is _____

because _____.

The way I feel about most of the kids at school is _____

_____.

Mostly, I think the kids at school _____
                                        (how do they feel about you)

because _____.

The way I feel about my teacher this year is _____

because _____.

The best teacher I ever had was _____.

He/She was so good because _____.

The worst teacher I ever had was _____

because _____.

My favorite subject is _____.

I like it so much because _____.

A subject I could improve in is _____.

I feel this way because _____ .

If I had the choice, I _____ go to school.
(would or would not)

Instead of school, I would _____ .

My teacher _____ know that I live in a single parent family.
(does, does not)

The way that _____ found out is _____ .
(he/she)

The parent who usually attends parent/teacher conferences is _____ .
(which parent)

The way I feel about this is _____

because _____ .

_____ kids at school also live in single parent families.
(About how many)

At school, when we have to make special things for my parent I don't live with, I feel _____

because _____ .

When I have special programs and activities at school, I invite _____
(whom)

to attend. Usually _____ attends. I feel _____
(who)   (how)

about this because _____ .

I think that the people in charge at my school _____
(understand/don't understand)

about living in a single-parent family. I think this way because _____

_____ .

The way I feel about this is _____

because _____ .

Getting Around

I go to school by _____ .
(what mode of transportation)

I feel _____ about getting to school that way because
(how)

_____ .

_____ gets around by _____ .
(My parent)   (what mode of transportation)

_____ - _____ getting around that way because
(He/She)   (how does he/she feel)

_____ .

One other person who takes me places is _____ .

_____ feels _____ about me going with that person
(My parent)   (how)

because _____ .

If I could go anywhere with anyone I'd like to, I'd go _____

_____ with _____ .
(whom)

The way I get to most special places is _____ .
(how)

If I could change one thing about getting to the places I go to, I would change _____

_____ .

If _____ could change one thing about how we get around, _____
(my parent)   (he/she)

would change _____

because _____ .

The World Around Us

The way I feel about living in the world is _____

_____ .

I feel this way because _____ .

The way _____ feels about living in the world is _____
        (my parent)

_____

_____ feels this way because _____ .
(My parent)

The best thing about the world is _____ .

The best thing about the world to _____ is _____
                                  (my parent)

_____

The worst thing about the world is _____ .

If I could, I would make this bad thing better by _____

_____

The worst thing about the world to _____ is _____
                                   (my parent)

_____ .

If _____ could, _____ would make this bad thing better
   (my parent)   (he/she)

by _____ .

Something I can do every day to make the world a better place to live is _____

_____ .

Something _____ can do every day to make the world a better place to live
          (my parent)

is _____ .

The world looks like this to me. . .